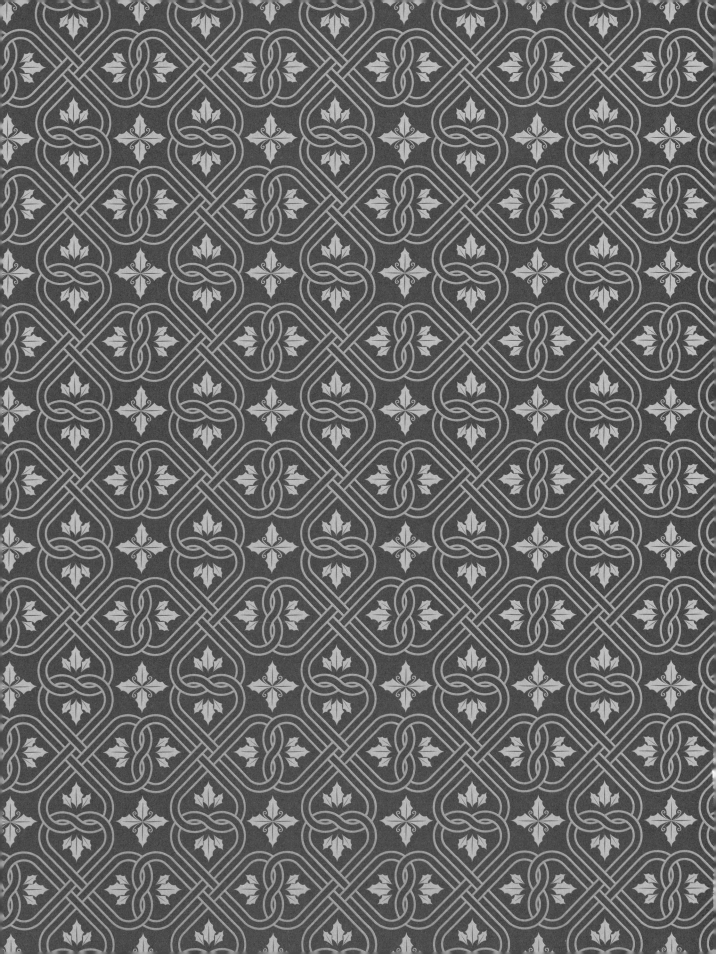

COME TO HIM
THIS HOLY NIGHT

OTHER BOOKS IN THE TABERNACLE CHOIR CHRISTMAS SERIES

Silent Night, Holy Night: The Story of the Christmas Truce • As narrated by Walter Cronkite

A Christmas Bell for Anya • As narrated by Claire Bloom

I Heard the Bells on Christmas Day • As narrated by Edward K. Herrmann

In the Dark Streets Shineth: A 1941 Christmas Eve Story • Written and narrated by David McCullough

Good King Wenceslas • As read by Jane Seymour

Christmas from Heaven: The True Story of the Berlin Candy Bomber • As read by Tom Brokaw

God Bless Us, Every One! The Story behind "A Christmas Carol" • As read by John Rhys-Davies

The Little Match Girl • As narrated by Rolando Villazón

It Is Well with My Soul • As narrated by Hugh Bonneville

Keepsake Christmas Stories: Holiday Favorites as Performed with The Tabernacle Choir • Featuring 13 Guest Narrators

For contributions to this book, the Choir expresses its thanks and appreciation for the following: copy editing, Lisa Mangum and Derk Koldewyn; music copy work, Steve Smith; music review, Rachael Ward and Tracy Keck; book design, Sheryl Dickert Smith; art direction, Richard Erickson; cover art, David T. Warner; legal coordination, Carol Newton for the Choir and Jack Newman and Michelle Spiron for Shadow Mountain; guest artist coordination, Ron Gunnell, Global Envoy for the Choir Presidency; product direction, Chris Schoebinger at Shadow Mountain and Scott Barrick, Choir General Manager; and executive direction: Michael O. Leavitt, Choir President, L. Whitney Clayton, First Counselor, and Gary B. Porter, Second Counselor.

The Tabernacle Choir at Temple Square provides artistic expressions of faith from The Church of Jesus Christ of Latter-day Saints.

Visit us at shadowmountain.com. Visit the Choir at TheTabernacleChoir.org.

Library of Congress Cataloging-in-Publication Data

Names: Warner, David T. (David Terry), 1963– author. | McDonough, Neal, writer of preface. | Warner, David T. (David Terry), 1963–
    illustrator. | The Tabernacle Choir at Temple Square.
Title: Come to him this holy night : three Irish Christmas traditions / The Tabernacle Choir with Neal McDonough ; written and
    illustrated by David T. Warner.
Description: Salt Lake City : Shadow Mountain, [2022] | Includes bibliographical references. | Summary: "A picture book written and
    illustrated by David T. Warner, including elements of the spoken-word and choral performances of the 2021 Christmas concert of
    The Tabernacle Choir at Temple Square, featuring Neal McDonough"—Provided by publisher.
Identifiers: LCCN 2022014397 | ISBN 9781639930609 (hardback)
Subjects: LCSH: Christmas—Ireland. | Ireland—Social life and customs. | BISAC: RELIGION / Holidays / Christmas & Advent |
    LCGFT: Picture books. | Gift books.
Classification: LCC GT4987.467 .W37 2022 | DDC 394.266309417—dc23/eng/20220429
LC record available at https://lccn.loc.gov/2022014397

Printed in China
RR Donnelley, Dongguan, China

10   9   8   7   6   5   4   3   2   1

COME TO HIM
THIS HOLY NIGHT

Three Irish Christmas Traditions

As performed by

THE TABERNACLE CHOIR

with Neal McDonough

Written and Illustrated by David T. Warner

SHADOW MOUNTAIN PUBLISHING

THE TABERNACLE CHOIR AT TEMPLE SQUARE

I was thrilled for the invitation to narrate The Tabernacle Choir's annual Christmas concert, but I wasn't prepared for the first time I heard the Choir and Orchestra live. Beyond their magnificent, world-class sound, it was readily apparent that they believe in the message of their music. I could feel it. As a result, being onstage with them was more than performing. It was collaborating with friends who care about the birth, life, and mission of Jesus Christ as I do.

This book presents the script for a special "Christ-centered" moment near the end of the concert, including narration about three Irish Christmas traditions and words for a new Christmas song, "Come to Him This Holy Night," written to the tune of a famous Irish folk song. In the concert performance, Broadway star Megan Hilty joined the Choir for the first and last verses, and the Orchestra provided an inspiring underscore. For readers who want to sing this song with family and friends, a simple piano accompaniment is provided at the end of the book.

As I explained to the live audience, the concert's Irish theme had special meaning for me. I grew up a devout Irish Catholic just outside of Boston, Massachusetts. My parents emigrated from Ireland in the late 1940s and early 1950s, met each other here, and raised us six kids with a great love for our homeland. So, even though my wife, Ruvé, is from South Africa and our five children were born in Los Angeles, we're never far from my Irish heritage, for which I am grateful.

In joining members of the Choir and Orchestra, I was especially humbled by the opportunity to strengthen the bridge between us—between my faith and theirs, and between God's children everywhere. I know He loves us. Each one of us. And I cherish the privilege of coming together with brothers and sisters from all over the world, to remember and worship His Son, Jesus Christ, at Christmastime.

—NEAL McDONOUGH

For generations, three Irish traditions have helped families welcome the Christ Child at Christmas—a prepared home and heart, a candle in the window, and a wreath of holly.

May these sacred traditions help you and your family welcome Jesus Christ into your lives, now and throughout the coming year.

Come to Him this holy night,

Though a Child in swaddled clothing

In a manger, none supposing

He is Christ the Lord, all knowing.

Come to Him this holy night . . .

A Prepared Home and Heart

I n Ireland, holiday preparations have included cleaning the barn, whitewashing the cottage, scrubbing floors, ironing linens, and cooking a special meal for family members coming home. As the Irish love to say, *níl aon tinteán mar do thinteán féin*— "there's no place like your own hearth," or, in other words, there's no place like home. And that's especially true at Christmas.

Today, families on the Emerald Isle still get ready for Christmas in some of the traditional ways. But their most important preparation has to do with their hearts—with remembering others, reconciling differences, and returning kindnesses. Even the old Irish custom of a Christmas morning dip in the icy sea is an invitation to wash away the old and begin anew—to welcome the Christ Child into hearts made clean and pure for Him.

Dress the cottage, sweep the floor,

Make Him room among us living,

For His love and sweet forgiving

And the hope of ever-living.

Dress the cottage, sweep the floor . . .

A Candle in the Window

One Irish Christmas tradition that has spread across the world is placing a candle in the window. It recalls the Holy Family seeking shelter but finding no room in the inn. For many, lighting a candle to shine in the darkness is an assurance that Mary and Joseph would have been welcome in their homes. It is also a sign that the poor, the weary, and the downtrodden can find refuge within.

Of course, light in the darkness is also a symbol of the Christ Child himself, the Light of the World. Today, whether it's a candle in the window or a light in our eyes, Christmas is a time to signal our willingness to love and serve those in need—sometimes in our homes and always in our hearts.

Light a candle, trim it bright,

Set it in the window shining

For the lonely one who's pining,

Seeking bread and milk for dining.

Light a candle, trim it bright . . .

A Wreath of Holly

In towns and villages across the island, the Irish live simply. But that doesn't keep them from decorating their homes for Christmas. And the most universal decoration is available to rich and poor alike. It's the humble holly bush, with its thorned leaves and bright red berries.

In earlier times, children would be sent out to scour the hills for holly branches, which would then be fashioned into a traditional wreath and hung on the wooden cottage door. It made perfect sense back then, for holly is a symbol of the Holy Child—the Child who would one day wear a crown of thorns, and whose drops of blood would symbolize His sacrifice for all humankind.

That sharp crown and those crimson droplets are a reminder that none of us suffer alone. And for believers in Christ, it is an assurance that He was born to heal, comfort, and redeem us from the sorrows of life. This is perhaps the most comforting symbol of all—that the Spirit of Christmas is the spirit of healing and hope, making the holidays truly holy days, now and all year through.

Gather holly on the lea,

See the thorny leaves concealing

Droplet berries, each revealing

In His suff'ring there is healing.

Gather holly on the lea . . .

THANKS BE TO GOD

Answering a tax decree from Caesar Augustus, Mary and Joseph returned to Bethlehem, the homeland of their ancestors. As prophesied, while they were there, "the days were accomplished that [Mary] should be delivered. And she brought forth her firstborn son, . . . and laid him in a manger; because there was no room for them in the inn" (Luke 2:7). It was an incomparable event. But, if their experience was even remotely like the experience most parents have when a child is born, joy is not a strong enough word to convey the feelings in their hearts.

Which is why at Christmas we sing joy to the world. For the symbol of a newborn baby is a reminder that Christmas is an opportunity for all of us to begin again—to walk in a newness of life ourselves. For which we say, *buíochas le Dia*—"thanks be to God," for all of His blessings, especially the blessings of Christmas.

Gaze upon this precious sight,

For He'll not be long in sleeping.

Give your soul to Him for keeping

And your sorrow for His weeping.

Gaze upon this precious sight . . .

For He's here with you tonight,

With the hosts of heaven singing

Let your songs of joy be ringing,

Bowing low and humbly bringing

Praise to Him this holy night!

COME TO HIM THIS HOLY NIGHT

David T. Warner

Irish Folk Song – "Wild Mountain Thyme"
arr. Mack Wilberg

Simply, but with expression (♩ = 72)

Him this ho-ly night, Though a Child in swaddled cloth-ing___ In a
cot - tage, sweep the floor, Make Him room a-mong us liv-ing___ For His
can - dle, trim it bright, Set it in the win-dow shin-ing___ For the
hol - ly on the lea, See the thor - ny leaves con - ceal-ing___ Drop-let
- on this pre-cious sight, For He'll not be long in sleep-ing,___ Give your
here with you to - night, With the hosts of heav-en sing-ing___ Let your

man - ger, none sup - pos-ing___ He is Christ the Lord, all know-ing.___ Come to
love and sweet for - giv-ing, And the hope of ev-er - liv-ing.___ Dress the
lone - ly one who's pin-ing, Seek-ing bread and milk for din-ing.___ Light a
ber - ries, each re - veal-ing, In His suff - 'ring there is heal-ing.___ Gath-er
soul to Him for keep-ing And your sor - row for His weep-ing.___ Gaze up-
songs of joy be ring-ing,___ Bow-ing low and hum-bly bring-ing___ Praise to

Come to Him This Holy Night (continued)

Please visit TabChoir.org/ComeToHim to watch the full concert performance narrated by
Neal McDonough with The Tabernacle Choir and Orchestra at Temple Square.

CHRISTMAS WITH THE TABERNACLE CHOIR

Every December, one of the many wonders of Christmas in Salt Lake City is the annual concert of The Tabernacle Choir and Orchestra at Temple Square, a Temple Square tradition for decades. Since 2000, these popular concerts have delighted live audiences of over 60,000 people each year in the Conference Center of The Church of Jesus Christ of Latter-day Saints, with millions more tuning in to *Christmas with The Tabernacle Choir* on PBS through the partnership of GBH and BYU Television. It is a full-scale production featuring world-class musicians, soloists, dancers, narrators, and music that delights viewers each year.

Each concert has featured a special guest artist, including Broadway actors and singers Megan Hilty, Kelli O'Hara, Kristin Chenoweth, Sutton Foster, Laura Osnes, Santino Fontana, Alfie Boe, and Brian Stokes Mitchell; opera stars Rolando Villazón, Deborah Voigt, Nathan Gunn, Renée Fleming, Bryn Terfel, and Frederica von Stade; Grammy Award–winner Natalie Cole, *American Idol* finalist David Archuleta; and The Muppets® from *Sesame Street*®. The remarkable talents of award-winning actors Neal McDonough, Richard Thomas, Hugh Bonneville, Martin Jarvis, John Rhys-Davies, Jane Seymour, Michael York, and Edward Herrmann have graced the stage, sharing memorable stories of the season. Featured narrators also include famed broadcast journalist Tom Brokaw, two-time Pulitzer Prize–winning author David McCullough, and noted TV news anchorman Walter Cronkite.

The 360 members of The Tabernacle Choir represent men and women from many different backgrounds and professions and range in age from twenty-five to sixty. The Orchestra at Temple Square includes a roster of more than 200 musicians who accompany the Choir on broadcasts, recordings, and tours. The Bells at Temple Square, a 32-member handbell choir, adds a particular sparkle to the concerts each year. All serve as unpaid volunteers with a mission of sharing inspired music that has the power to bring people closer to the divine.

The Tabernacle Choir's weekly *Music & the Spoken Word* program is the longest-running continuous broadcast in history. Five of the Choir's recordings have achieved "gold record" and two have achieved "platinum record" status. Its recordings have reached the #1 position on *Billboard*® Magazine's classical lists a remarkable fifteen times since 2003. Today, music from the Choir and Orchestra is available through the Choir's YouTube channel, Spotify, Apple Music, Amazon Music, and Pandora. For more information about these Christmas concerts and available performance videos, please visit TabChoir.org/ComeToHim.

NEAL McDONOUGH

Neal McDonough is a multi-talented, award-winning actor who has been seen in over 100 films, including the award-winning Christian film *Greater* (2016), *Captain America* (2014), *Forever Strong* (2008), and *The Warrant* (2020) and major television dramas, including as Lt. Compton in *Band of Brothers,* many seasons as Sean Cahill in *Suits,* and as General Harding in Robert Zemekis's *Project Blue Book.* McDonough has appeared onstage as Daddy Warbucks in *Annie* and in the title role in *Willy Wonka and the Chocolate Factory.* Born to Irish parents and raised in Dorchester, Massachusetts, Neal is a devout Catholic. His most prized accomplishments are his relationships with his wife, Ruvé, their five children, and with God.

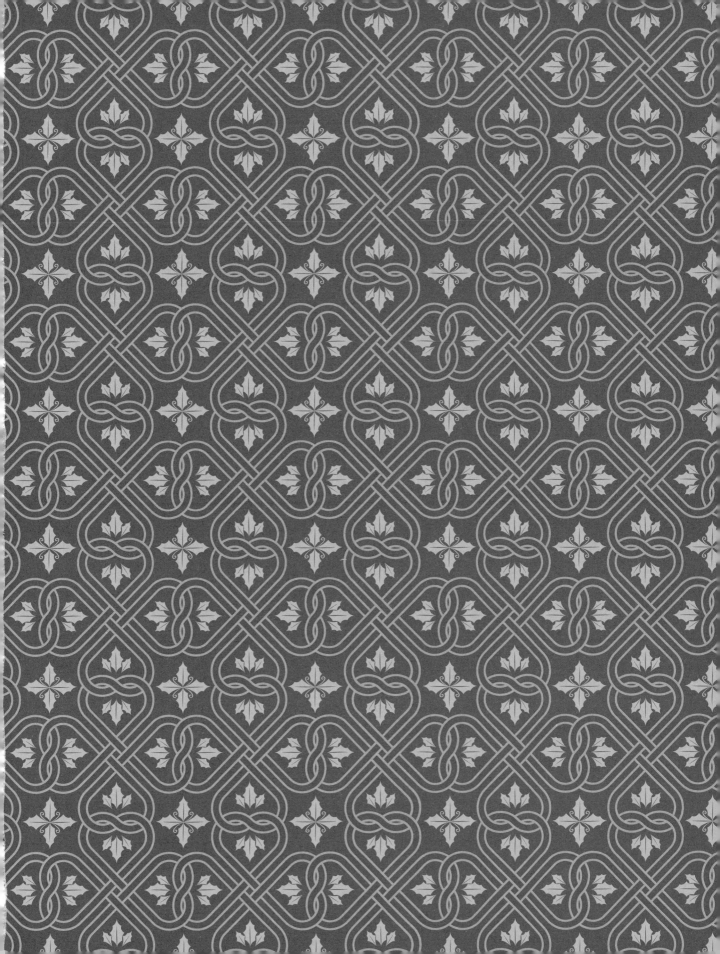

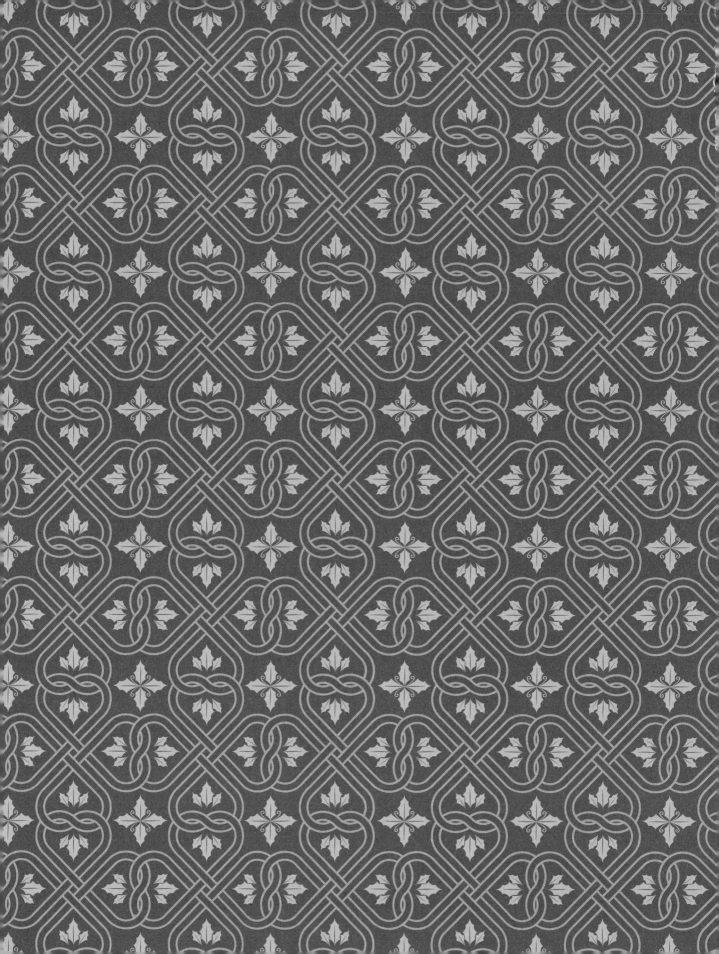